Who Was Richard Nixon?

by Megan Stine

illustrated by Manuel Gutierrez

Penguin Workshop

For you—MG

PENGUIN WORKSHOP
An Imprint of Penguin Random House LLC, New York

Visit us online at www.penguinrandomhouse.com.

Library of Congress Control Number: 2019034744

ISBN 9781524789800 (paperback)   10 9 8 7 6 5 4 3 2 1
ISBN 9781524789817 (library binding)   10 9 8 7 6 5 4 3 2 1

Contents

Who Was Richard Nixon?

Washington, DC

On August 8, 1974, the most powerful man in the world was crying. President Richard Nixon was about to go on TV. At nine o'clock that night, he was going to announce to the nation that he would resign from the presidency. He had been caught in a terrible scandal. Congress was talking about putting him on trial. There was even a chance he could go to prison.

Nixon had spent his whole life trying to be strong, bold, and brave. He said he never cried—not in public or in private. He never even let his wife or children see his emotions. But now he was crying so much, the makeup person could hardly get him ready for television.

Just two years earlier, Richard Nixon had been reelected as president in a landslide victory. He won in every single state except Massachusetts. What had happened since then to make a president leave the White House in disgrace?

Richard Nixon (right) with Vice President Spiro Agnew

The answer is the story of Watergate—a scandal that rocked the nation. It is a story of spying and wiretapping—and then covering it all up with money and lies. It is a story about men who committed serious crimes in order to win an election.

But most of all, it is the tragic story of one man—Richard Nixon—who wanted to be good and wanted to achieve great things for America but somehow lost his way.

CHAPTER 1
Small Boy, Big Ideas

Richard Milhous Nixon was born on January 9, 1913, on a small farm in Yorba Linda, California. His mother, Hannah, was very strict. She didn't think it was right to drink alcohol, dance, or swear. All his life, Richard would call his mother a saint. But she was a quiet, cold woman who never showed her children much affection.

Nixon family, 1917

Richard's father, Frank, was the opposite. Frank Nixon had never gone to high school. He was a loud man who bullied his sons. But he loved to discuss politics with young Richard.

Richard had four brothers. Two of them died young from illnesses. Richard, the second oldest, was extremely smart. His teachers skipped him ahead from first grade to third.

He also loved music from an early age. He took piano and violin lessons, and he later learned to play the clarinet, saxophone, and accordion.

When the family farm failed, the Nixons moved to Whittier, California. Richard was nine at the time. His father opened a gas station and grocery store in town. Every day before school, Richard had to get up at four to buy vegetables for the store.

In high school, Richard got excellent grades. He tried hard to fit in. But he was shy, clumsy, and not very popular.

The one thing Richard excelled at was public speaking. He was a star of the debate team. In

a debate two people take opposing sides in discussing an important issue. He also had a part in the school play.

After high school, Richard was accepted at one of the best colleges in the country—Harvard University. But his family couldn't afford it. So Richard stayed home and attended Whittier College instead. The students from the richest families belonged to a club called the Franklin Society. When Richard tried to join it, the Franklins rejected him.

Hurt by being snubbed, Richard formed his own club. In those days, black students were almost never accepted in clubs run by white students. But Richard's club made sure everyone was welcome.

After graduation, Richard got a full scholarship to attend Duke University School of Law in North Carolina. The beautiful buildings on campus looked like castles to him. He didn't live

Duke University School of Law

in a fancy dorm, though. He lived in a shack with no heat and no bathroom!

Richard had to work hard in law school. And he graduated in the top of his class.

Nevertheless, when he went to New York City to apply for a job, all the best law firms turned him down. Why? He hadn't gone to an Ivy League school—like Harvard or Yale. Once again, Richard was being snubbed. He never got over how it felt to be rejected by one group and then another.

In 1937, Richard went home to Whittier and fell into a slump. Now what? How could a smart young man make a name for himself if no one would give him a chance?

CHAPTER 2
Toughening Up

Richard Nixon was a fighter at heart, so pretty soon he was back on his feet. Nixon believed that it didn't matter how many times he got knocked down. What mattered was getting up again.

He got a job at a law firm in Whittier. In a little more than a year, he was a partner with his name on the door. He became well known in town and well respected.

For fun, he got involved with an amateur theater group. One day, he saw a beautiful redhead named Pat Ryan. Richard fell in love with her and asked her out on a date.

"I'm very busy," Pat said.

"You shouldn't say that," Richard joked, "because someday I am going to marry you!"

Pat just laughed. She kept turning him down. But he wouldn't give up. In time, they started dating. Sure enough, on June 21, 1940, they were married.

In December of the next year, the Japanese bombed Pearl Harbor, Hawaii. It meant that the United States was going to war.

Richard and Pat Nixon moved to Washington, DC. He had lined up a job working for the government. But after eight months, Richard Nixon wanted to do more than just sit at a desk. He wanted to help the United States win World War II.

So Richard joined the Navy as an officer. Eventually, he was sent to an island in the South Pacific. His job was to take care of supplies for bomber pilots.

He was good at his job. He even managed to get some extra supplies for the men. Nixon set up a hamburger stand with free beer and burgers. His nickname was "Nick" Nixon, so he called it Nick's Hamburger Stand. (Later, Richard would be called "Dick" by all who knew him.)

World War II (1939–1945)

Adolf Hitler

World War II started in 1939 when Nazi Germany invaded Poland. England and France declared war on Germany two days later. Germany was led by Adolf Hitler, who wanted to take over Europe. The war spread beyond Europe to Africa.

At the same time, Japan was at war with China. (Japan was also an ally of the Nazis.) America didn't join the war until Japan bombed American ships in Pearl Harbor on December 7, 1941. World War II ended in early September 1945.

Pearl Harbor attack, 1941

As a boy, Richard had never drunk liquor, smoked, or used curse words. And he certainly didn't bet on card games. But in the Navy, he was no longer so strict with himself. He began to swear like the other men. He drank a little. And he became so good at poker, he won thousands of dollars.

Finally, in September 1945, the war was over.

A few weeks later, Richard got a letter from an important businessman back home. Would Richard like to come back to California and run for Congress as a Republican?

Of course he would! Richard loved politics. Here was a good place to start. That was, if Pat agreed. And she did.

Once back in California, Richard worked hard to learn everything about politics. He also took advice from Murray Chotiner, a political adviser. Chotiner told Richard to get "dirt"—embarrassing information—on his opponent, Jerry Voorhis. Richard couldn't find any dirt on Voorhis, so he bent the truth instead. When he debated Voorhis, Richard twisted the facts to make it sound like Voorhis was in favor of things he was actually against. It was a sneaky, underhanded way to win the debate.

Republicans and Democrats:
What's the Difference?

Democratic donkey   Republican elephant

Today there are two main political parties in the United States. Their members hold different views on how the country should be governed. Republicans believe in fewer government programs and lower taxes. Democrats believe that having more government programs and higher taxes for wealthy Americans can help the poor. Republicans are called conservatives and Democrats are called liberals.

In February, after the Nixons' first daughter, Tricia, was born, Pat plunged into the campaign. She attended almost every rally.

On November 5, 1946, Richard was elected to Congress. He later wrote that he and Pat were happier about this victory than they would ever be again in his whole career.

CHAPTER 3
Life in Washington

When he got to Washington, Richard was given the worst office a congressman could get. It was in the attic! But he was seen as one of the bright young stars among the new congressmen. Another was a good-looking first-year Democratic congressman from Massachusetts. His name was John Fitzgerald Kennedy.

John was rich, glamorous, and worldly. Plus, he had a Harvard degree. He was everything that Richard was not.

That first year in Washington, Dick and Pat Nixon were invited to a

John Fitzgerald Kennedy

fancy party at the home of a wealthy member of Congress. They didn't know what to wear. When they showed up, the Nixons weren't nearly as dressed up as everybody else.

Still, the congressmen at the party were impressed with young Richard. They chose him to be part of a group traveling to Europe to talk to world leaders. After the trip, they would advise Congress about the country's relationship with Europe now that the war was over. This was what Richard wanted most of all. He loved foreign affairs—making decisions about how the United

States should deal with other countries.

The committee sailed to Europe on a huge ocean liner called the *Queen Mary*. Richard had tea with the prime minister of England. He toured all the major capital cities of Europe and saw the damage World War II had done. Many cities were still in rubble. He also saw that many people were hungry and out of work.

By the time he came home, Richard was convinced that the United States should help Europe get back on its feet. He voted in favor of giving money—foreign aid—so the European countries could rebuild. Richard thought it was the right thing to do. He also believed it was the best way to stop the spread of communism.

In Congress, there was a committee whose main job was to investigate Americans who might be communist spies. It was called the House Un-American Activities Committee— HUAC for short. HUAC, however, went way overboard looking for communists. They accused many Hollywood celebrities and others of being "Reds"—a nickname for communists. HUAC demanded that these people rat on their friends. Many people's careers were ruined. It was a shameful time in American history.

At the end of 1947, Richard was appointed to HUAC. He was brought in to make sure the committee followed the law and caught some *real* spies. He grew famous for going after a man named Alger Hiss. Hiss was a model citizen. He worked high up in the government. No one could believe he was a Russian spy.

Alger Hiss

Communism

Communism is a system of government based on the idea that everyone should share the wealth. There shouldn't be any rich people or any poor people. In communist countries, individual people don't own businesses—everything is owned by the government. Communism is the opposite of capitalism—the system we use in the United States. With capitalism, people own the businesses. Some people get rich while many workers remain poor.

In the 1930s and '40s, many smart, educated people in the United States joined the Communist Party. They thought the system seemed fair. Most Americans, though, were against communism. Russia was a communist country—and Russia was taking over other countries to form the Union of Soviet Socialist Republics (USSR, or Soviet Union). Americans feared that the Soviets might want to take over the United States someday. By the late 1940s and '50s, many people thought that anyone in the United States who was a communist was un-American.

Richard thought Alger Hiss was lying. He questioned Hiss during hearings that were held on TV. Richard was like a dog with a bone, who wouldn't give it up.

In the end, Hiss was found guilty of lying under oath—perjury—which is a crime. He went to jail for more than three years. His reputation was ruined.

But in some ways, Richard Nixon's reputation was damaged, too. Sure, everyone knew who Richard Nixon was. But many Washington insiders—especially liberals who had gone to Ivy League schools—thought Richard was on a witch hunt and had ruined Hiss's life unfairly.

What was the truth about the Alger Hiss case? To this day, experts aren't sure. But there is a lot of evidence that Richard was right. Alger Hiss may have been passing secrets to the Russians.

That year—1948—was a big year for the Nixons in another way, too. Pat gave birth to their second child, Julie. Now their family was complete.

But the excitement wasn't over.

Richard Nixon's life in the spotlight was just getting started.

CHAPTER 4
Scandal

Now that he was famous, Richard Nixon wanted greater things for himself. Being a congressman was satisfying work. Being a US senator would be even better.

In 1950, he decided to run for the Senate in California.

His Democratic opponent was a woman named Helen Gahagan Douglas. He called her "the Pink Lady." By that, he meant she might be a "Red," or a communist. He thought calling her that would help him win votes.

Helen Gahagan Douglas

But Helen came up with a mean nickname for Nixon, as well. She called him "Tricky Dick." It stuck with him for the rest of his life.

During the campaign, Richard drove ten thousand miles all over California to meet with voters. Pat went with him. On election night, Richard won by more than twenty points—a huge win. He celebrated by playing the piano at all the victory parties.

But back in Washington, DC, Richard was still unpopular with the in-crowd. They wouldn't forgive him for being a "Red hunter"—chasing after supposed communists. Cartoonists made fun of Richard in the newspaper. And at one dinner party, a rich, famous Democrat walked out when he saw that Richard was a guest.

So Richard kept mostly to himself. He had only a couple of close friends. One of them was Bebe Rebozo. Bebe lived in Florida and took Richard fishing. The other close friend was his secretary, Rose Mary Woods. She was like a part of the family. She became very close to Pat.

In the summer of 1950—before even winning his Senate seat—Richard was invited to Bohemian Grove. Bohemian Grove was a huge, secret men's campground in Northern California. The members of the club included the richest and most powerful men in the world. They met every year in July to have fun. Sometimes they discussed political deals, too.

That year, Dwight
D. Eisenhower came
to Bohemian Grove.
Eisenhower had been
an important general
during World War II.
He was a national hero.
Eisenhower—"Ike"

Dwight D. Eisenhower

for short—was planning to run as the Republican
candidate for president in 1952. He was looking
for someone to be his vice president.

Could Richard Nixon be the one? Bohemian
Grove was a chance for Ike to look Richard over.
And Nixon seemed to pass the test.

As time went on, the two didn't exactly get
along—but it didn't matter. Ike needed Richard as
an "attack dog" on the campaign trail, going after
his opponents. So he chose Richard to run as his
vice president. Richard did his job. He attacked

Ike's opponent, calling him a "waltzing mouse." He also called the Democratic president a traitor. Even some of Richard's supporters thought he had gone too far.

Then suddenly, in September 1952, Richard Nixon was under attack.

The *New York Post* ran a story that said he had a secret fund of more than $18,000. Rich Republicans had given him the money. The article made it sound like Richard used the money to buy expensive things—and owed the rich people favors in return.

The story was not fair. Wealthy donors *had* given money to Richard Nixon's campaign. But Richard wasn't spending it on expensive clothes or jewelry. He was using it to travel around the country, getting people to vote for Ike.

Still, the story created a scandal. Crowds began to heckle Richard at campaign rallies. They threw coins at him as if to say, "Here—take our money, too!"

Within a few days, newspaper articles and Ike's advisers were calling for Richard to quit the ticket. He got the feeling Ike wanted him gone, too.

Should he quit? Richard was a fighter, and so was Pat. Pat told him not to give up.

Then some other Republican leaders came up with an idea. They told Richard to go on TV and give a speech to the country, explaining everything.

On the night of September 23, 1952, Richard made a speech on NBC Television. Television was still very new in 1952. Most people didn't own a TV. Still, nearly half the country watched Richard or heard him on the radio.

In the speech, Richard explained that he and Pat weren't rich. They lived very simply, Richard said, even borrowing money from his parents. He explained that Pat didn't have a mink coat—only a "respectable Republican cloth coat."

At the end of the speech, he admitted that he had accepted one gift as a politician. It was a black-and-white cocker spaniel puppy named Checkers. A man in Texas had sent it when he heard that Richard's daughters wanted a dog. Richard ended by saying his family planned to keep the dog, no matter what anyone said.

The TV speech became known as the Checkers speech.

When it was over, the NBC cameramen were crying. And the phones at NBC started ringing. People from all over the country called and sent telegrams. They were almost all in favor of Richard!

Once Ike saw how the public reacted, he was happy. He rushed to meet Richard on a plane. "You're my boy!" Ike said.

When the election was held that November, Ike and Richard won in a landslide.

The day he was sworn in as vice president, Richard's mother gave him a note. It said she was

proud of him. She also told him to remember to stay true to his religion—that, for his mother, was the most important thing of all.

Richard kept the note in his wallet for the rest of his life.

CHAPTER 5
The World Stage

Richard Nixon had always wanted to deal with other world leaders. Now, as vice president, it was his job to do just that.

Ike sent his young vice president to Asia in 1953. At home in the United States, Richard still seemed awkward around people, but overseas, he was very popular. Leaders in foreign countries thought he was charming. They also liked that Richard treated them with respect.

In 1956, President Eisenhower and Richard Nixon won a second term in the White House. It was another landslide victory.

Two years later, Ike sent Richard on another important trip—this time to Latin America. It was supposed to be a "goodwill" tour to show

The Eisenhowers and the Nixons

different countries that the United States was their friend.

The trip was a terrible experience. Many Latin American countries were beginning to hate the United States. Student protesters filled the streets. They shouted and threw rocks at Richard and spit in his face. Why? Because the American government had tried to overthrow the governments of certain Central American countries. And companies from the United States were trying to take over in the region.

The police told Vice President Nixon to stay away from the angry crowds. But Richard never backed down from a fight. So he plunged into

the crowds in Peru. He tried to speak calmly to the protesters. It worked for a moment. Then someone threw a rock. It hit a Secret Service agent's face—a man who was protecting the vice president. When another man spit at Richard, Richard kicked him in the shins!

In Venezuela, the protests were worse. As he and Pat arrived at the airport, the crowds spit on them from a balcony. At first, Richard thought it was raining. Then he realized that gobs of spit were landing on his clothes. He and Pat hurried into a limousine and tried to drive away. But

they couldn't escape. The road was blocked with hundreds of people surrounding the car. Protesters threw rocks and smashed the glass with crowbars. They rocked the car back and forth, trying to turn it over. Richard thought he and Pat were going to die.

But when a Secret Service agent took out his gun, Richard stopped him. He told the Secret Service not to shoot unless they dragged him out of the car—and even then, "only if I tell you."

Finally, they were able to drive away to safety.

When Pat and Richard Nixon returned to the United States, they were greeted like heroes. President Eisenhower went to the airport himself. So did all the leaders of government and about fifteen thousand other people. Everyone admired how well Richard had handled a dangerous situation.

But Richard's biggest foreign trip was still yet to come. In 1959, Ike sent Nixon to Moscow, Russia, to meet Nikita Khrushchev, the nation's communist leader. Americans were a little bit afraid of Khrushchev

Nikita Khrushchev

because he had once said, "We will bury you." Khrushchev meant that communism would win out over American capitalism.

Richard prepared for the trip the way he had always prepared for debates—by studying. Only this time, he studied for six months! When he met Khrushchev in person, he was able to argue calmly and coolly about the American way of life.

Richard was so happy, he had a few drinks that night. Then he and Khrushchev both threw their vodka glasses into the fireplace. *Smash!* It's what Russians often did at big celebrations.

The Cold War

The decades-long tension between the United States and the Soviet Union was known as the Cold War. There were no actual battles, but the two nations were enemies. There was always the danger of a real war breaking out—one that might be fought with atomic bombs. The Cold War ended in 1991 when the Soviet Union collapsed.

After the trip to Moscow, Richard was more popular in America than ever. He was on the cover of *TIME* magazine.  He was only forty-six years old. It seemed like Richard Nixon was heading to become the next president of the United States.

What could possibly go wrong?

CHAPTER 6
Loser

Richard Nixon and John F. Kennedy had known each other a long time. And although they were political opponents, the two men had never been enemies. John had invited Richard and Pat Nixon to his wedding. The next year, John was dangerously sick in the hospital. Richard had

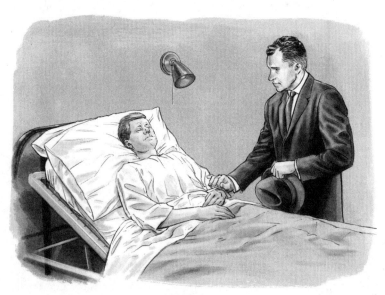

gone to see him. Richard was so shaken by the visit, he left almost in tears.

But in 1960, they were running against each other to be the next president of the United States.

Richard knew that John would be tough to beat. John was a popular senator from Massachusetts. He believed that government should do more to help people in need. He also had a glamorous young wife, a beautiful little girl, and a million-dollar smile. However, he was Catholic. In those days, some people thought a Catholic president might be more loyal to the Pope than to the United States.

Jacqueline Kennedy

Richard decided the best way to beat John was by working harder. He announced that he would visit every one of the fifty states during his campaign. It was a grand promise. It also turned out to be a terrible mistake.

Why? Richard had agreed to debate John—on television. The presidential debates had never been televised before. Millions of people would watch. It could swing the election one way or the other.

But right before the first debate, Richard had been racing around the country, trying to keep his campaign promise. He visited twenty-five states in just fourteen days. On the trip, he injured his knee and was hospitalized for two weeks. By the time the debates came along, Richard was exhausted and losing weight. He looked terrible.

John, on the other hand, looked healthy, relaxed, and tan. He spent the time before the first debate resting and listening to music.

Nearly half the country watched the debates on TV—more than seventy million people. Many thought Richard did a good job answering the questions. But he looked bad and was sweating under the hot TV lights.

Also, John was willing to play dirty tricks on his rivals, just as Richard had. John spread around money, paying people to get out the vote on election day.

But the biggest reason John did so well was that he won over black voters. In October 1960, right before the election, Dr. Martin Luther King Jr. was arrested in Atlanta. He was taken to jail in handcuffs after a protest for civil rights. John called Coretta Scott King, Dr. King's wife, to show his concern—and let the newspapers know he had called her. Then John's brother Robert worked behind the scenes to get Dr. King released.

Dr. Martin Luther King Jr. arrested in 1960

Richard, on the other hand, didn't speak up. He said nothing about Dr. King's arrest. He had always believed in equal rights, but he was afraid of losing votes from racist white southerners. His silence hurt him in the election.

Election Day was November 8. It was going to be a close one. Not all votes were counted till early the next morning. More than sixty-eight million votes were cast nationwide. John won by only a little more than one hundred thousand votes. It was so close.

The New York Times.

KENNEDY'S VICTORY WON BY CLOSE MARGIN;
HE PROMISES FIGHT FOR WORLD FREEDOM;
EISENHOWER OFFERS 'ORDERLY TRANSITION'

Richard was bitter about losing. Some people thought he should challenge the results. Even President Eisenhower thought so. But Richard wanted to lose like a gentleman, with dignity. He told Kennedy he wouldn't put up a fight.

Two years later, Richard was asked to run for governor of California. He agreed, but his heart wasn't in it. He lost the election to a Democrat named Pat Brown.

The next morning, Richard went to a hotel ballroom where the press was gathered. He made a short speech. It was a speech that would be famous for years to come. He said to the reporters, "Just think how much you're going to be missing. You don't have Nixon to kick around anymore—because, gentlemen, this is my last press conference."

It seemed like Richard Nixon was quitting politics for good.

CHAPTER 7
Comeback

In 1963, Richard and Pat Nixon moved to New York City. He started practicing law again. He was making much more money. They lived in a beautiful apartment.

Richard said he would never run for office again. And most people thought if he did run, he would never win. But the world was about to

Lyndon B. Johnson

change in ways no one could have foreseen.

In 1963, President John F. Kennedy was shot and killed in Dallas, Texas. Vice President Lyndon B. Johnson took over as president. The next fall, Johnson ran for the presidency in his own right and won in a landslide.

Soon after that, the war in Vietnam heated up—and that changed everything.

By 1965, Richard was getting antsy. He began to make lists on yellow legal pads. It was a lifelong habit. On his birthday in 1965, he made a list of New Year's resolutions. First on the list was "Set great goals."

He probably knew right then that he wanted to run for president again.

In 1967, to get ready for the next election, Richard began to travel around the world. He wanted to meet the world leaders who were in charge now. His favorite was Charles de Gaulle, the president of France.

Charles de Gaulle

The Vietnam War

The war in Vietnam began in 1954 and lasted twenty years. At first, it was a war between North and South Vietnam. Then communist countries joined in to help North Vietnam. The United States entered the war to stop the spread of communism

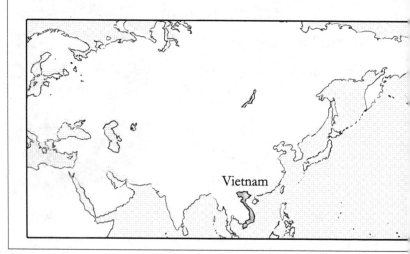

Vietnam

and help South Vietnam.

By the late 1960s, people in the United States were very divided between those in favor of the war and those against. As President Johnson kept sending more troops to fight, college students protested. Why were we fighting a war half a world away? By 1970, most Americans thought the war had been a mistake.

In the end, America did not win in Vietnam, and fifty-eight thousand American soldiers—and three million Vietnamese—died.

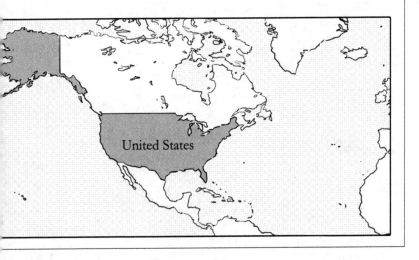

De Gaulle had given Richard some important advice. He told Richard to "open" China. At that time, China was a closed, communist country. It did not have any contact with Europe or the United States. De Gaulle said if the United States became friendlier with China, it would take power away from Russia. It would be a smart move.

But first, Richard would have to win the election.

The 1968 presidential election campaign was filled with drama and tragedy.

First, the drama: President Johnson shocked America by saying he wouldn't run again. The

tragedy was the assassination of JFK's brother Robert F. "Bobby" Kennedy. He had stepped in to try to win the Democratic nomination for president. But he was shot in a hotel in Los Angeles. He died the next morning. The whole nation grieved.

With Bobby Kennedy dead, the nomination was up for grabs. Protesters showed up in Chicago at the Democratic National Convention. That was where the Democrats would choose their candidate for president. The protesters were peaceful, but the mayor of Chicago wanted them

Robert "Bobby" Kennedy, 1968

gone. Police with riot gear and tear gas came at protesters. There was chaos in the streets with hundreds injured.

In the end, Hubert Humphrey, who had been Johnson's vice president, was chosen to be the Democratic candidate. That's who Richard would have to beat. Richard made a campaign promise that if he won, he would end the war in Vietnam.

Then Richard put together a team of men to help him get elected. One of them was H. R. Haldeman. He was picked to run the campaign. Richard told Haldeman that the campaign was "an all-out war." In other words, Haldeman could use plenty of dirty tricks to win.

On election night, the results came in slowly, as usual.

Finally, at eight thirty the next morning, Richard was declared the winner over Humphrey, although not by much.

Richard Nixon was thrilled. He went home

to his apartment on Fifth Avenue in New York. Then he opened the windows wide and put on some music—his favorite. It was a piece from *Victory at Sea*. Richard wanted everyone to hear the triumphant music on the streets outside.

In January 1969, he was sworn into office and the Nixon family moved into the White House. That night, he asked the White House staff to turn on every single light in the whole mansion. It was his way of celebrating. It was also his way of announcing to Washington, DC, that Richard Nixon was back and here to stay.

CHAPTER 8
President!

Before Richard Nixon went to sleep in the White House for the first time, he peeked under the bed. There was a nest of wires and cables underneath. Some were hooked up to recording equipment—Lyndon Johnson had had the White House bugged. Richard told his staff to tear all of that stuff out. Then he got to work on the things that mattered most to him.

He toured the world again to meet with foreign leaders. He especially wanted to talk to Charles de Gaulle. Richard hoped to start peace talks in Paris that would end the war in Vietnam.

Meanwhile, antiwar protesters often stood outside the White House chanting and yelling. They held up signs. Richard could hear them from his bedroom. He knew they blamed him for not ending the war.

In the middle of the protests late one night, Richard decided to drive to the Lincoln Memorial. He took a personal staff member, Manolo, with him. The memorial houses a larger-than-life statue of Abraham Lincoln. At night, it is lit up.

Lincoln Memorial

Richard walked up the steps at five in the morning, just before the sun was coming up. Student protesters were gathered there. They were shocked to see the president of the United States appear out of the blue.

Richard tried to explain to them that he was doing the best he could to end the war. He explained that he hated war. But when the newspapers heard about the story, they reported that Richard was foolish and out of touch. They made fun of Richard and said he had ignored what the protesters wanted to talk about.

Unlike the protesters, most of the people in the country thought Richard was doing a good job. Richard called those people the "Silent Majority." He meant that most of the country didn't speak up—they were silent—but they approved of him. In some ways, Richard was right.

During his first four years, Richard did many positive things for the country. He created the

First Earth Day celebration, 1970

Environmental Protection Agency (the EPA) to keep the environment safe. He signed new versions of the Clean Air Act and the Clean Water Act. He also passed laws to keep workers safer and healthier on the job. He started a War on Cancer to help scientists find a cure for the disease. And he made sure that schools were desegregated. That meant black children and white children would attend the same schools.

In June 1971, Tricia Nixon got married in the Rose Garden at the White House. It was a joyful event—one of the happiest times of Richard's first four years.

Elvis at the White House

On December 21, 1970, a famous rock 'n' roll singer showed up at one of the guardhouse gates at the White House. It was Elvis Presley! He wanted to see the president. Richard decided to let him in. Elvis had brought a gift for the president—a loaded gun! But the Secret Service took it away from him. Elvis said he wanted to be a narcotics agent in the War on Drugs—and he wanted a narc badge. Richard agreed to give him one. Then Elvis hugged him, and they had their picture taken together.

Out of the public's view, Richard was also working to open a relationship with China. He asked Henry Kissinger, one of his top advisers, to get secret messages to the Chinese leaders offering to have talks. Finally, in 1972, Richard Nixon made the trip to China. He was the first American president ever to visit China and offer to begin trading with the communist country. Many people around the world praised Richard for this brave, bold move.

Richard with Communist Party Chairman Mao Zedong in China, 1972

Later that year, Richard went to Moscow to meet with the Soviet leaders. It was the first time an American president had visited Russia's capital city.

Still, Richard was hated by the Washington insiders—the press, many longtime politicians, and especially the Democrats. He was mocked in the newspapers. More and more, he kept to himself. Many nights, he ate dinner alone. He refused to see members of Congress. He lashed out at people and lost his temper more often.

He also began to keep a list of enemies. He wanted to get back at them. Some were senators. Others were reporters and newspaper owners.

Richard turned to his closest staff members for help. H. R. Haldeman was now his chief of staff. John Ehrlichman was an assistant to the president. Rose Mary Woods was still his trusted secretary and friend.

In 1971, Richard Nixon asked them to set up a taping system so he could record conversations in the White House. He also got the FBI (Federal Bureau of Investigation) to bug the phones of four news reporters—and thirteen people on his own White House staff!

And that was only the beginning. Tricky Dick was just getting started.

CHAPTER 9
Dirty Tricks

When Richard started spying on his enemies, he had to know it was wrong. It is against the law to use the government's spying power on people who haven't committed crimes. Yet Richard asked Haldeman and Ehrlichman to figure out a way to spy on the hippies and antiwar protesters who spoke out against him. And he wanted the IRS—the government tax agency—to go after his enemies by looking at their tax returns. Richard claimed that Presidents Kennedy and Johnson had done the same thing to him and to his friends. Now it was his turn to get even.

IRS symbol

Haldeman and Ehrlichman were pretty much running the White House. They knew that sometimes the best plan was to ignore whatever the president asked them to do. Richard was known for being hotheaded at times. He would give an order, then change his mind the next day.

Unfortunately, not everyone knew it was okay to ignore the president's orders. John Dean, a young lawyer at the White House, wasn't aware of that. And neither were three other men who had been brought in to do dirty tricks. Their names were G. Gordon Liddy, E. Howard Hunt Jr., and Chuck Colson.

Liddy had been in the FBI. He loved to talk about violence. Sometimes, he would put his

John Dean

G. Gordon Liddy

hand in a flame to prove how tough he was.

E. Howard Hunt Jr. had worked at the CIA (Central Intelligence Agency), which handled spying missions overseas. Hunt, however, was sort of a bumbler. The CIA had wanted to get rid of him.

Chuck Colson was an ex-marine who couldn't wait to pull some dirty tricks.

Together Liddy, Hunt, and Colson came up with wild schemes they thought Richard would like. Liddy wanted to kidnap war protesters, drug them, and take them to Mexico! He and Hunt also spied on JFK's brother, Senator Ted Kennedy.

They got into trouble when they tried to help Richard with a famous case called the Pentagon Papers.

E. Howard Hunt Jr.

Chuck Colson

In 1971, Daniel Ellsberg took some secret papers from the Pentagon, where he had worked,

and gave them to the *New York Times*. The Pentagon Papers showed that US presidents had been lying to Americans about winning the war in Vietnam.

Richard tried to stop the newspaper from printing the story. He took the *Times* to court. But the Supreme Court said the president was wrong to interfere with freedom of the press. Newspapers were allowed to print the Pentagon Papers.

After that Liddy and Hunt came up with a dirty trick against Ellsberg. They broke into Ellsberg's psychiatrist's office to find out secrets about him.

Richard didn't know about most of the dirty tricks in advance. And he didn't give his approval. But he had asked Haldeman and Ehrlichman to do a lot of illegal things—including spying on Democrats. No one knew when to say no or how to stop.

In 1972, the dirty tricks spread to the election that was coming up that November. Richard was running for his second term as president. His opponent was Senator George McGovern. Richard wanted to be sure of victory. His staff knew that he was okay with them playing dirty tricks on the Democrats.

George McGovern

So Haldeman approved giving money from the reelection campaign to Liddy and Hunt. Three hundred thousand dollars! They could use it however they wanted.

On the night of May 26, 1972, Richard Nixon

was in Moscow talking to the Russians. At the same time, G. Gordon Liddy and E. Howard Hunt Jr. were in Washington, DC, at the Watergate Hotel.

Watergate complex

They were planning a crime that would ruin not only Richard Nixon's presidency, but Americans' faith in their government.

CHAPTER 10
Watergate

The plan was to send burglars to break into the headquarters of the DNC, the Democratic National Committee. The DNC offices were in the Watergate complex. That's where Democrats ran the presidential campaign for George McGovern.

The burglars were supposed to plant bugs on the office phones so Richard's team could listen to everything the DNC said. They thought this would help win the election. But the burglars were clumsy spies. It took them four tries before they managed to bug the phones. And before they got out, a security guard caught them and called the police. Soon, the burglars were arrested.

Hunt and Liddy had been watching the

burglars from a hotel room across the street. When they saw the police arrive, they fled. But they were in such a rush, they left behind some clues—papers with Hunt's name on them.

The Watergate break-in was reported in the newspapers. At first, Richard wasn't worried. He hadn't asked Hunt and Liddy to commit this crime. And he didn't think it could be tied to him.

But little by little, more details came out. The FBI began to investigate. So did reporters from the *Washington Post*. Soon it became clear that people who worked in the White House—Richard's closest advisers—were involved. They might not have known about the Watergate break-in in advance, but they knew soon after. And they all lied about it to cover it up.

Richard himself wasn't sure what to do. One minute, he said that they should come clean and tell the truth. He knew cover-ups were a mistake. The next minute, he told Haldeman to find a way to shut down the FBI investigation.

Meanwhile, the election was nearing. Richard was way ahead of McGovern in the polls. Everywhere Richard went, people chanted and cheered, shouting, "Four more years!"

On November 7, the country voted to keep Richard in the White House for a second term. He won by one of the biggest landslides in history.

The Watergate scandal seemed to fade into the past.

Except it didn't. Two reporters from the *Washington Post* were still working on it. Bob

Bob Woodward and Carl Bernstein

Woodward and Carl Bernstein kept trying to find the truth. The more they reported in the newspaper, the more it looked like President Nixon might have been involved. How could his staff members be spending campaign money *without* Richard knowing about it?

In January 1973, the Watergate burglars were put on trial. They were all found guilty and sent to jail. But the judge made an unusual statement at the end. He said he thought other people in the White House were also involved. In a way, he was pointing a finger at the president.

Eventually, the truth leaked out. John Dean started talking. He told the government prosecutors that Haldeman had a secret fund of hush money—money he was paying to the burglars to keep them quiet. Pretty soon, it was clear that Haldeman and Ehrlichman were part of the cover-up, too.

President Nixon forced Dean, Haldeman, and Ehrlichman to resign. If they took the blame, maybe Richard would be safe.

But firing them wasn't enough to save Richard's presidency.

In May 1973, a special prosecutor was appointed—a man named Archibald Cox. His job was to find out the whole truth about Watergate. That same month, the Senate began to hold hearings. The hearings were broadcast on TV all day for thirty-seven days. Millions of Americans watched them.

One day, a shocking piece of information came out. An assistant to the president revealed that there was a secret recording system at the White House. It recorded all the conversations Richard had in the Oval Office.

Instantly, the special prosecutor wanted to hear those tapes.

Richard didn't want the public—or anyone—to hear them. He thought about erasing them, but he didn't. Maybe the tapes would prove that he was innocent?

For months, Richard refused to give the tapes to Archibald Cox. Finally, a court said Richard *had* to turn them over. Instead, Richard decided to get rid of Cox! He ordered the two top men in the Justice Department to fire Cox. Both men refused. They resigned rather than do it. It became known as the Saturday Night Massacre. A massacre is when a lot of people are wiped out at once.

When the public heard what President Nixon had done, they guessed he had something to hide. Voters turned against him.

Meanwhile, a new special prosecutor was appointed to replace Cox. His name was Leon Jaworski. He wanted to hear the White House tapes, too.

In November 1973, President Nixon held a press conference. He told reporters, "I'm not a crook."

In July 1974, the Supreme Court ruled that Richard had to turn over the tapes. But eighteen minutes of the sound had been erased. Richard's loyal secretary, Rose Mary Woods, said she had "accidentally" erased them.

In any case, the tapes showed that Richard and

Haldeman had tried to cover up the truth about the Watergate burglaries. Worse yet, they revealed Richard talking about crushing his enemies at any cost. He talked nastily about Jewish people and black people. He sounded like a person no one could like or admire.

Worst of all, the tapes proved that Richard had committed a crime. He told John Dean to go ahead and use the hush money. Hunt was paid $75,000 to keep quiet. Richard also told

Haldeman to get the FBI to drop the case. Both of those things were against the law. They were obstruction of justice, which means "preventing justice."

Three days later, a committee in the House of Representatives took the first steps to impeach President Nixon.

Richard didn't want to be impeached. It would be humiliating. Instead, he chose to resign.

On August 8, 1974, he appeared on TV to announce he was leaving. Before the speech, he had been weeping while his TV makeup was

applied. After the speech, he went upstairs in the White House to hug his family. He was so upset, his whole body shook.

The next day at noon, President Nixon walked out of the White House for the last time. Before he left, he made a speech to the staff, saying, "Always give your best, never get discouraged, never be petty." Then he and his family stepped into a helicopter that was waiting to take them away.

Richard turned at the last minute to wave goodbye to the crowds. He threw both his arms up and made a *V* with his fingers. It was the *V* for victory that Ike had used during World War II. But it was also the peace sign that hippies and protesters had always used.

No one thought Richard Nixon was leaving in victory or peace.

That day, Vice President Gerald Ford took over as president.

Impeachment

Impeachment is the way presidents and other government officials can be removed from office if they commit crimes or abuse their power. Impeachment starts when the House of Representatives votes to put someone on trial. The trial itself is held in the Senate. The Senate votes as to whether the person is guilty and must leave office.

Andrew Johnson was the first president to be impeached. Bill Clinton was the second. Neither was voted out of office. In December of 2019, Donald Trump became the third president to be impeached.

Bill Clinton

Donald Trump

President Ford soon decided to pardon Richard for any crimes he may have committed. That meant Richard would not be brought to trial. President Ford wanted the whole messy era of Watergate to be over so the country could move on.

But the men who had followed Richard's orders and covered up Watergate were never pardoned. Haldeman, Ehrlichman, Colson, and more than a dozen others spent time in prison.

Richard Nixon spent the last twenty years of his life trying to repair his reputation. In 1977, he did a series of interviews with a talk show host named David Frost. Millions of people watched.

Richard wrote nine books during the last part of his life. He also traveled around the world, gave speeches, and met with foreign leaders. He wasn't exactly beloved or forgiven after the disgrace of Watergate. But he wasn't hated quite as much, either.

Former US presidents Clinton, H. W. Bush, Reagan, Carter, Ford, and the former first ladies attend Nixon's funeral

In 1994, Richard Nixon had a stroke. He died four days later on April 22.

President Bill Clinton spoke at his funeral. All the former presidents attended it. Thousands of people waited for hours to walk past his casket and pay their respects. The line was more than three miles long!

When he was buried, a sentence from Richard Nixon's first inaugural speech was carved on his tomb. It said: "The greatest honor history can bestow is the title of peacemaker."

Perhaps, by the end of his life, Americans had made peace with Richard Nixon at last.

Timeline of Richard Nixon's Life

1913	Richard Milhous Nixon is born in California
1937	Graduates from Duke University School of Law
1940	Marries Pat Ryan
1946	The Nixons' first daughter, Tricia, is born
	Elected to Congress as a Republican from California
1948	Accuses Alger Hiss of being a communist spy
	The Nixons' second daughter, Julie, is born
1952	The Checkers speech is broadcast on TV
	Elected vice president of the United States
1956	Reelected for second term as vice president
1959	Meets the communist leader Nikita Khrushchev in Moscow
1960	Runs for president against John F. Kennedy and loses
1962	Loses race for governor of California
1968	Elected president of the United States
1970	Creates the Environmental Protection Agency
1972	Makes an historic trip to Beijing, to open US relationships with China
	The Watergate break-in occurs at the Democratic National Committee headquarters
1974	Resigns from the presidency
1994	Dies at the age of eighty-one

Timeline of the World

1912	The *Titanic* sinks in the Atlantic Ocean
1914	World War I begins in Europe
1920	The Nineteenth Amendment that gives women the right to vote is ratified
1929	US stock market crashes
1939	Nazis invade Poland, starting World War II
1945	World War II ends
1954	Vietnam War begins
1957	Soviet Union launches Sputnik
1963	Dr. Martin Luther King Jr. makes his "I Have a Dream" speech
	President Kennedy is assassinated in Dallas, Texas
	Lyndon B. Johnson becomes president
1968	Dr. Martin Luther King Jr. is assassinated
	Robert Kennedy is assassinated
	Riots break out at the Democratic National Convention in Chicago
1969	United States lands a manned spacecraft on the moon
	The Woodstock music festival is held
1975	The war in Vietnam ends
1989	The World Wide Web is invented
1991	The Soviet Union collapses as communism is overthrown

Bibliography

*Books for young readers

Carlson, Peter. "When Elvis Met Nixon." *Smithsonian*, December
2010. https://www.smithsonianmag.com/history/when-elvis-
met-nixon-69892425/.

Farrell, John A. *Richard Nixon: The Life*. New York: Doubleday,
2017.

Klein, Christopher. "The Last Hours of the Nixon Presidency."
History.com, August 8, 2014. https://www.history.com/news/
the-last-hours-of-the-nixon-presidency-40-years-ago.

Nixon, Richard. *RN: The Memoirs of Richard Nixon*. New York:
Simon & Schuster, 2013.

Thomas, Evan. *Being Nixon: A Man Divided*. New York:
Random House, 2016.

*Tracy, Kathleen. *The Watergate Scandal*. Hockessin, DE:
Mitchell Lane Publishers, 2007.

P9-CQB-310

DANIEL BOONE

by Laura K. Murray

PEBBLE
a capstone imprint

Pebble Explore is published by Pebble, an imprint of Capstone.
1710 Roe Crest Drive
North Mankato, Minnesota 56003
www.capstonepub.com

Library of Congress Cataloging-in-Publication Data
Names: Murray, Laura K., author.
Title: Daniel Boone / Laura K. Murray.
Description: North Mankato, Minnesota : Pebble, an imprint of Capstone, [2021] | Series: Biographies | Includes bibliographical references and index. | Audience: Ages 6–8 | Audience: Grades 2–3 | Summary: "How much do you know about Daniel Boone? Find out the facts you need to know about this pioneer and explorer in early America. You'll learn about the early life, challenges, and major accomplishments of this famous American"—Provided by publisher.
Identifiers: LCCN 2020030661 (print) | LCCN 2020030662 (ebook) | ISBN 9781977132055 (hardcover) | ISBN 9781977133076 (paperback) | ISBN 9781977154071 (ebook)
Subjects: LCSH: Boone, Daniel, 1734–1820—Juvenile literature. | Explorers—Kentucky—Biography—Juvenile literature. | Pioneers—Kentucky—Biography—Juvenile literature. | Frontier and pioneer life—Kentucky—Juvenile literature. | Kentucky—Biography—Juvenile literature. | Cumberland Gap (Ky. and Va.)—Discovery and exploration—Juvenile literature. Classification: LCC F454.B66 M87 2021 (print) | LCC F454.B66 (ebook) | DDC 976.9/02092 [B]—dc23
LC record available at https://lccn.loc.gov/2020030661
LC ebook record available at https://lccn.loc.gov/2020030662

Image Credits
Alamy: Chronicle, 26, Pictures Now, 15; The Art Institute of Chicago: Karl Bodmer, Deliverance of the Daughters of Daniel Boone and Callaway, 1852, Gift of Dorothy Braude Edinburg to the Harry B. and Bessie K. Braude Memorial Collection, 19; iStockphoto: bauhaus1000, 22; Library of Congress: Photographs in the Carol M. Highsmith Archive, 16; Newscom: Ken Welsh, 21; North Wind Picture Archives: 5, 7, 8, 11, 12, 29, Gerry Embleton, 10; Science Source: 14; Shutterstock: Jim Vallee, 25, Nagel Photography, 23, Olena Rodina (geometric background), cover, back cover, 2, 29; Smithsonian Institution: National Portrait Gallery, partial gift of the William T. Kemper Foundation and of the Chapman Hanson Foundation, cover, 1, 20; Wikimedia: U.S. Navy, 24

Editorial Credits
Editor: Erika L. Shores; Designer: Elyse White; Media Researcher: Svetlana Zhurkin; Production Specialist: Spencer Rosio

All internet sites appearing in back matter were available and accurate when this book was sent to press.

Table of Contents

Words in **bold** are in the glossary.

Who Was Daniel Boone?

Daniel Boone was a hunter and explorer. He led the way for people to move west during the 1700s. At that time, America was growing in size.

In Daniel's time, most white **settlers** lived on the East Coast. Daniel found new ways to go west. He made a path called the Wilderness Road. American Indians had lived on the land for many years.

There are many **folk stories** about Daniel. But not all of them are true.

Growing Up

Daniel was born November 2, 1734, in Berks County, Pennsylvania. Pennsylvania was one of the 13 **colonies** ruled by Great Britain.

Daniel was the sixth of 11 children. Growing up, he spent most of his time outside. He helped on the family's farm. He explored the woods. He went hunting and fishing. Daniel did not go to school. But his aunt taught him to read and write.

a colonial family by their log cabin in Pennsylvania

a hunter carrying home a turkey

Daniel was a good hunter. He learned to hunt with a long, pointed stick called a spear. Around age 12, his father gave him a rifle. Daniel hunted deer, turkeys, and other animals for his family to eat.

Daniel learned from the American Indians who lived nearby. They taught him about hunting and tracking animals. Around the time Daniel was 16, his family moved to North Carolina. The move took more than a year.

Fighting and Hunting

In 1754, the French and Indian War began. Daniel joined the North Carolina army. He and the colonists were on the side of the British. The French and some groups of American Indians were on the other side.

British soldiers and colonists fought French soldiers and American Indians in 1755.

Colonists worked on their small farms and hunted in the nearby woods.

After the war, Daniel went home to North Carolina. He married Rebecca Bryan on August 14, 1756. Daniel and Rebecca had 10 children. Daniel made money by hunting, trapping, and farming.

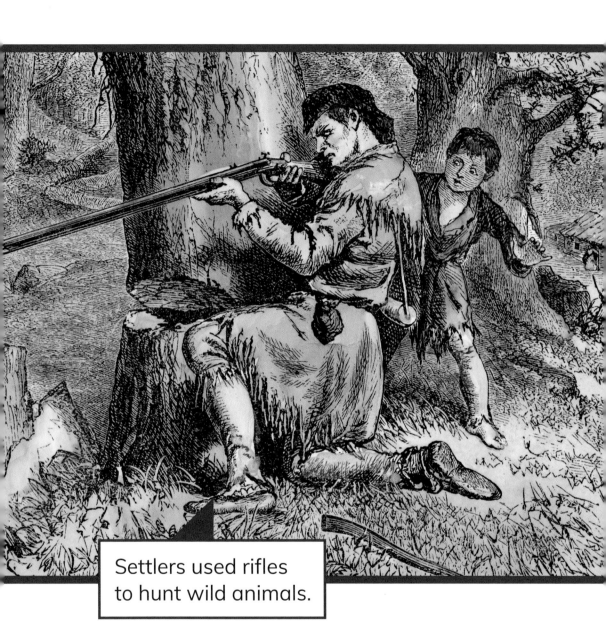

Settlers used rifles
to hunt wild animals.

Soon, problems started between the colonists and the Cherokee people. In 1759, the two groups fought. The Boones and other families moved to Virginia to stay safe. Daniel served in the North Carolina army during this time.

Three years later, the Boones went back to North Carolina. But it was hard for Daniel to earn money. Many new settlers had moved to the area. There were not as many animals left to hunt. Daniel looked for a new place to live. He traveled to Florida. But he decided not to move there.

Wilderness Road

In 1767, Daniel saw Kentucky for the first time. Kentucky was part of Virginia. The land was full of deer, bears, and other animals. Two years later, Daniel went to Kentucky again. Daniel and another hunter were captured by the Shawnee people. They told the hunters to never come back to their lands. Daniel did not listen.

The Shawnee captured Daniel and his friend.

Daniel and his family
moved many times.

In 1773, the Boones and other
families decided to move to Kentucky.
On the way, American Indians fought
to keep them out. Daniel's son James
and others were killed. The families
went back to North Carolina.

Daniel and his group arrived in Kentucky in 1775.

Settlers kept moving into the hunting lands of American Indians. In 1774, colonists and American Indians fought. Daniel was in charge of **forts** in Virginia. After the colonists won, they took over American Indian lands.

The next year, a company hired Daniel to make a trail into Kentucky. People wanted it to be a new colony. Boone led a team to clear a path through the Cumberland Gap. The path was called the Wilderness Road. It became a way for settlers to go west. Daniel's group also built a fort called Boonesborough.

Going West

Daniel was an army leader during the **Revolutionary War** (1775–1783). He and the colonists fought to be free from British rule.

In 1776, Cherokee and Shawnee Indians kidnapped Daniel's daughter Jemima and her two friends. Daniel helped rescue them. A few years later, Daniel was captured too. A Shawnee leader made him part of the tribe. But Daniel escaped.

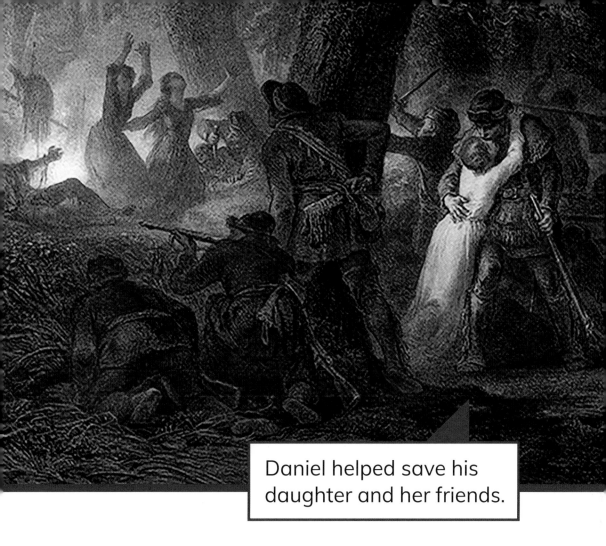

Daniel helped save his daughter and her friends.

During the war, Daniel also held **government** jobs. In 1782, he was made sheriff. The same year, Daniel's son Israel was killed in battle. America won the Revolutionary War in 1783.

In 1799, the Boones went farther west. Daniel was 65 years old. The family moved to Upper Louisiana. American Indians had lived there for many years. But the Spanish claimed the land as their own. By 1801, the land was owned by France.

In 1803, U.S. President Thomas Jefferson made a land deal with France. It was called the Louisiana Purchase. It nearly doubled the size of the country. The Boone family's land was part of the deal. Today, it is in Missouri.

Missouri was part of the Louisiana Purchase.

Daniel spent his later years with his family. He had money troubles. At times in his life, Daniel owned **enslaved** people. They were made to work without pay.

Daniel's grave in Kentucky

Daniel's son Nathan built a big house in Missouri. The family farmed, hunted, and grew food. Rebecca died in 1813. Daniel died on September 26, 1820. He was 85 years old.

Remembering Daniel

Today, some places in the United States are named for Daniel. Towns, schools, and parks have his name. There was a U.S. Navy submarine named after him.

The submarine USS *Daniel Boone* served from 1963 to 1984.

Daniel Boone National Forest

People can visit places from Daniel's life. The Daniel Boone National Forest is in Kentucky. People hike, hunt, and fish there. The Historic Daniel Boone Home is in Missouri. It is the home Nathan Boone built. Today, the Wilderness Road is part of U.S. Route 25.

Daniel became famous during his life. A book written in 1784 told about his adventures. People still tell stories about Daniel in books, movies, and poems. Some of the stories are tall tales. Many stories say Daniel wore a coonskin cap. But this is not true. Daniel liked to wear **felt** hats made out of beaver fur. They had wide brims.

Daniel Boone set out to explore new places. He had to solve problems on his own. He made new paths for others to follow. People will remember his love of adventure.

Important Dates

November 2, 1734 — Daniel Boone is born in Berks County, Pennsylvania.

1750 — Daniel's family moves to North Carolina.

1754 — Daniel fights on the British side during the French and Indian War.

August 14, 1756 — Daniel marries Rebecca Bryan.

1769 — Daniel is captured by the Shawnee in Kentucky.

1775 — Daniel helps clear a path to the west through the Cumberland Gap. It is called Wilderness Road.

1783 — American colonies win the Revolutionary War against the British.

1799 — Daniel and his family move to present-day Missouri.

1803 — The Boones' Missouri land becomes part of the U.S. with the Louisiana Purchase.

September 26, 1820 — Daniel dies in Missouri at age 85.

Fast Facts

Name:
Daniel Boone

Role:
explorer and hunter

Life dates:
November 2, 1734 to September 26, 1820

Key accomplishments:
Daniel Boone helped explore and settle parts of the American West. He helped make a trail called the Wilderness Road through the Cumberland Gap in the Appalachian Mountains. It became a main path people used to settle the West.

Glossary

colony (KAH-luh-nee)—an area that has been settled by people from another country and is owned by that country

enslave (en-SLAYV)—to make someone lose their freedom

felt (FELT)—a matted material

folk story (FOLK STOR-ee)—a legend or tale told and passed down from one group of people to the next

fort (FORT)—a place with strong walls where troops stay

Revolutionary War (rev-uh-LOO-shuhn-air-ee WOR)—the American colonies' fight from 1775 to 1783 for freedom from Great Britain

settler (SET-uh-lur)—a person who makes a home in a new place

Read More

Coutts, Lyn. *Explorers and Pioneers: Intrepid Adventurers Who Achieved the Unthinkable.* Hauppauge, NY: Barron's, 2018.

Raum, Elizabeth. *Cutting a Path: Daniel Boone and the Cumberland Gap.* North Mankato, MN: Capstone, 2016.

Internet Sites

Daniel Boone: PBS World Explorers
www.pbslearningmedia.org/resource/pbs-world-explorers-daniel-boone/

North Carolina Museum of History: Daniel Boone Legacy
www.ncmuseumofhistory.org/daniel-boone-legacy

The Historic Daniel Boone Home
www.sccmo.org/1701/The-Historic-Daniel-Boone-Home

Index